EMILY AKKERMANS

The WoNDERS of TiME

THE HISTORY AND MYSTERY OF TIME EXPLAINED

ILLUSTRATED BY **JAN BIELECKI**

WAYLAND

ROYAL
OBSERVATORY
GREENWICH

For James Atkinson – E. A.
For Mum and Dad – J. B.

First published in Great Britain in 2023 by Wayland
Text © National Maritime Museum, Greenwich, London 2023
Illustration and Design: © Jan Bielecki 2023

Editors: Grace Glendinning and Sarah Peutrill
Design & Illustrations: Jan Bielecki

Produced in association with Royal Museums Greenwich, the group name for the
National Maritime Museum, Royal Observatory Greenwich, Queen's House and *Cutty Sark*

www.rmg.co.uk

ISBN: 978 1 5263 1824 4 HBK
ISBN: 978 1 5263 1825 1 PBK
ISBN: 978 1 5263 2550 1 EBOOK

An imprint of
Hachette Children's Group
Part of Hodder & Stoughton

Carmelite House
50 Victoria Embankment
London EC4Y 0DZ

An Hachette UK Company
www.hachette.co.uk
www.hachettechildrens.co.uk

CONTENTS

WHAT IS TIME?

Time is a funny thing. A lot has been said about it:

It's an illusion!

It doesn't exist!

It flies when you're having fun!

But what *is* time? When did it begin and will it ever end? It's easy to take time for granted, but questions like these have fascinated scientists and philosophers for centuries.

TIME ON EARTH

Millennium	One thousand years
Century	One hundred years
Decade	Ten years
Year	365 days, or 366 days in a leap year
Month	The year is divided into 12 months
Week	7 days
Day	24 hours
Hour	60 minutes
Minute	60 seconds
Second	9,192,631,770 cycles of radiation of the caesium-133 atom
	See page 29 for more information on this!

Time is everywhere

Time plays a key role in things such as science and engineering today. We also use time to record events and to think about what *has been* and what's *to come*. We take time to sleep, eat, work and play.

Clocks, watches and smartphones are everywhere in the twenty-first century, but once upon a time we looked up at the Sun and other stars to tell us about time.

What *is* time, then?

Well, time is many things. It can be described as a series of events, running from past to future.

Time is also a measurement. This can be a long period of time – a year, a decade or a century – or a small period – hours, minutes or seconds.

What do *you* think about time?

Sometimes it seems as though hours pass like minutes; at other times, minutes seem more like hours. Usually this 'slow time' happens if you are doing something you don't like.

But did you know that your sense of time changes over the course of your lifetime?

When you are very young, time seems to last forever. Waiting a year between birthdays feels like an eternity. But as you get older, the years suddenly seem to pass swiftly.

The speed of time

German scientist Albert Einstein (1879–1955) came up with some groundbreaking ideas about time in the early twentieth century. His famous theory is now known as the theory of relativity. It sounds complicated but don't worry, all it means is that time passes slower the faster you travel. So, in theory, if you travelled faster than the speed of light, you would be able to go back in time!

Unfortunately, nothing can move faster than the speed of light. If we want to time travel, we will have to find another way.

THE BEGINNING OF TIME

One theory about time is that it started with the Big Bang, nearly 14 billion years ago, when the Universe exploded and started to expand. Not everyone agrees this was the dawn of time and we may never find out the real answer, but in this book, we will start our Universe timeline here.

Timeline of the Universe

13.6 billion years ago

About 13.8 billion years ago

Big Bang

The Milky Way is formed

A fast start

Before the Big Bang, the entire Universe was tiny, smaller even than a speck of dust, and it was incredibly hot. The Big Bang lasted only a fraction of a second, but the Universe has been expanding ever since and has cooled down a lot, too.

Over time, dust, gas and space rocks became the planets, moons, asteroids, comets, solar systems and galaxies of our Universe. Our galaxy, the Milky Way, was born about 13.6 billion years ago.

In terms of age, our Sun is only a young adult. Earth is slightly younger. Their ages aren't much in the grand scheme of time!

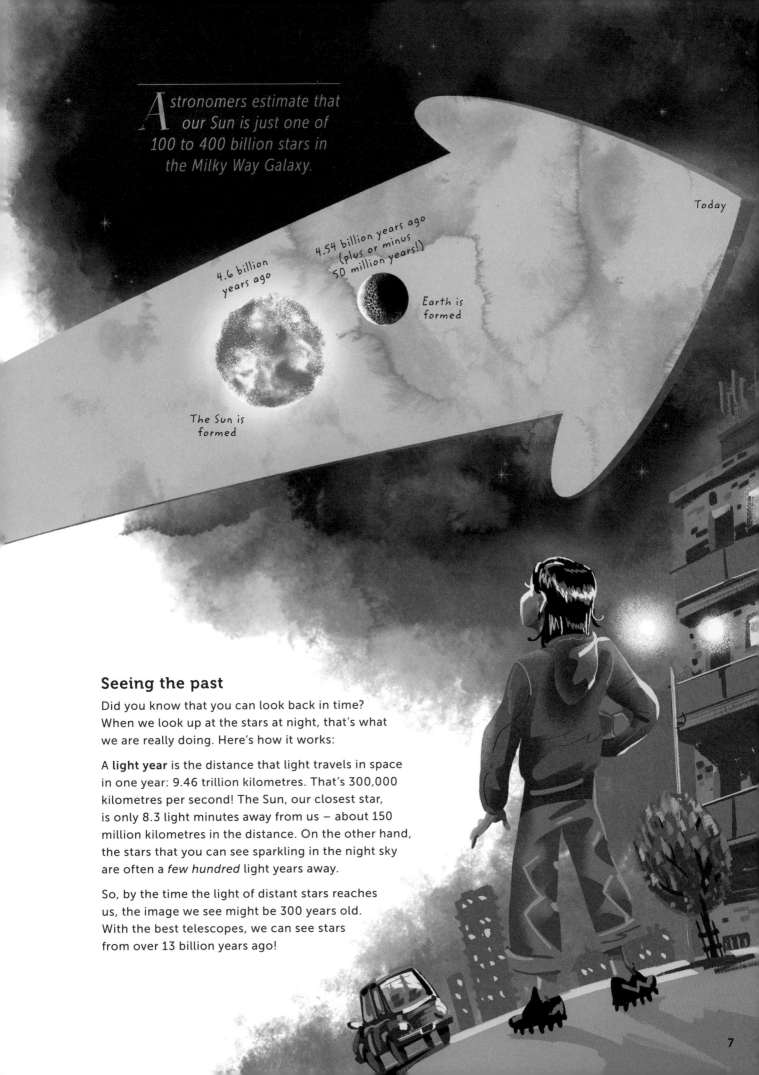

Astronomers estimate that our Sun is just one of 100 to 400 billion stars in the Milky Way Galaxy.

Today

4.6 billion years ago

The Sun is formed

4.54 billion years ago (plus or minus 50 million years!)

Earth is formed

Seeing the past

Did you know that you can look back in time? When we look up at the stars at night, that's what we are really doing. Here's how it works:

A **light year** is the distance that light travels in space in one year: 9.46 trillion kilometres. That's 300,000 kilometres per second! The Sun, our closest star, is only 8.3 light minutes away from us – about 150 million kilometres in the distance. On the other hand, the stars that you can see sparkling in the night sky are often a *few hundred* light years away.

So, by the time the light of distant stars reaches us, the image we see might be 300 years old. With the best telescopes, we can see stars from over 13 billion years ago!

7

THE SOLAR SYSTEM

If somebody asked you the time, you might look on your phone or at a clock. You could tell them the exact time, to the second. You could also tell them the exact date, including the day, month and year. But how did we get here? And what does the solar system have to do with it?

The Sun

Our Sun is the heart of our solar system and it is incredible. It is a hot, burning star made almost entirely of hydrogen and helium.

The Sun would be a deadly place to visit, as its hottest part is over 15 million degrees Celsius — or 27 million degrees Fahrenheit!

But without its heat and light, there would be no life on Earth. Our Sun is definitely the one in charge of our solar system. Its mighty gravitational force keeps Earth and the other seven planets firmly in their orbits.

With a diameter of 1.4 million kilometres, the Sun is very large indeed — about 10 times the size of Jupiter.

The motion of the cosmos

All the planets in our solar system orbit the Sun. But they also rotate on an axis, and it's both these movements that are important to humans. These rotations determine the length of a year on a planet and the number of days in that year.

Earth orbits the Sun on an elliptical, or egg-shaped, path.

A year on Earth is (roughly!) 365 days – the amount of time it takes Earth to orbit the Sun. We call this a solar year, which is the basis for the solar calendar (see page 16).

All the while, Earth is rotating on its axis. One spin of Earth takes about 24 hours, a period we call one day.

Jupiter's orbit

Mercury's orbit

Earth's orbit

Venus' orbit

Mars' orbit

North Pole

Winter in the northern hemisphere when it tilts away from the Sun

Polar Circle

Around the winter solstice, no sunlight reaches beyond the Polar Circle. That means the Sun never rises in the day! This is called the 'polar night'.

EARTH

The Tropic of Cancer

Earth's axis is tilted at 23.5 degrees relative to the Sun. It's because of this tilt that we experience changing seasons on Earth.

Equator

Sun's rays

The Tropic of Capricorn

Summer in the southern hemisphere when it tilts towards the Sun

Polar Circle

If you're beyond the Polar Circle around the summer solstice, the Sun doesn't set at night! This is called the 'polar day' or 'midnight Sun'.

South Pole

TIME IN SPACE

Planets in relative size to one another and the Sun:

The
Sun

Rocky planets:

• Mercury • Venus • Earth • Mars

Inner space

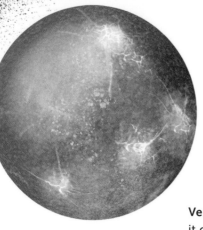

Mercury orbits the Sun much faster than our planet does: a year is only 88 Earth days. However, Mercury rotates very slowly. One day on Mercury is about 59 days on Earth, or 1,416 Earth hours.

Venus is perhaps the oddest planet when it comes to time. A year on Venus is about 224.7 Earth days. But Venus spins so slowly on its axis that one Venus day lasts 243 Earth days. A day on Venus is longer than its year. In other words, you would celebrate your first birthday on the same day that you were born!

Earth is about 150 million kilometres from the Sun. Astronomers call this distance 1 Astronomical Unit, or AU. AUs are used to measure other distances within our solar system.

A day on **Mars** is very similar to an Earth day. A Martian day is only 39 Earth minutes and 35 Earth seconds longer. But if you moved to Mars, you might struggle with the long, dark winter nights.

Planets in relative distance to each other and the Sun:

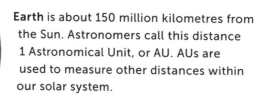

The Sun Mercury Venus Earth Mars   Jupiter   Saturn

1 AU 2 3 4 5 6 7 8 9 10 11 12 13 14

There are eight orbiting planets in total in our solar system: the inner rocky planets Mercury, Venus, Earth and Mars; the outer gas giants Jupiter and Saturn, and the ice giants Uranus and Neptune. Let's have a look at what time looks like on planets other than ours.

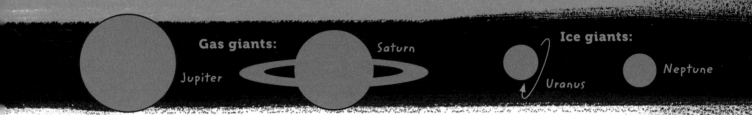

Gas giants:
Jupiter
Saturn

Ice giants:
Uranus
Neptune

Outer space

Jupiter is the biggest planet in our solar system. Jupiter takes 4,333 Earth days to orbit the Sun, or nearly 12 Earth years. A young teen on Earth would be just 1 year old on Jupiter.

Saturn, like Jupiter, has short days and long years. Saturn also has seasons because, like Earth, it is tilted on its axis.

Uranus is about 2.9 billion kilometres from the Sun. Uranus is different from all the other planets in the solar system: it rotates on its side! At its North Pole, a winter's night can last 21 Earth years.

Neptune is so far away that it takes about 165 Earth years to orbit the Sun. That means a year on Neptune is 60,190 Earth days! Your summer holiday on Neptune would last a whopping 15,047 days. But good luck finding a beach on Neptune – it's cold and windy, and doesn't even have a solid surface!

Which would you prefer – Jupiter's short days and long years, or Mercury's long days and short years?

View from
Earth's northern
hemisphere

New moon

Waning
crescent

Last quarter

Waning gibbous

Full moon

Waxing
gibbous

First quarter

Waxing
crescent

New moon

The Sun

Earth orbiting the Sun, and the Moon orbiting Earth, over 29.5 days

Humans have looked to the Sun for timekeeping for thousands of years. But other celestial bodies play a very important role, too.

MOON
AND THE
STARS

Lunar times

The Moon is what we call a natural satellite – a celestial body that orbits a planet, such as Earth. The Moon is our nearest neighbour in the Universe. Unlike the Sun, the Moon itself is very cold and does not emit any light or energy. Instead, what we see is the light of the Sun reflecting off the Moon's surface.

Every 29.5 days the Moon passes through eight phases. This is called a lunar month, which has an average of 29 or 30 days. One lunar year is made up of 12 lunar months, or about 354 days. This is the basis for the lunar calendar (see page 16).

OPHIUCHUS

Star times

The stars that we see are similar to our Sun, but so far away that we only see them as a little speck of light. In fact, they are so far away that they appear motionless. This is why we call them fixed stars. Humans have created maps of these stars, and use them to plot the position of the Sun and Moon as time passes.

The ecliptic (the curvy line you see below) is the path of the Sun in relation to the stars. You can draw a line through the stars along which the Sun appears to move during the year. (It is, of course, Earth that moves, but from our perspective here on Earth, we observe what's called the 'apparent motion' of the Sun.)

The Ecliptic follows a curved path because of Earth's 23.5 degree tilt.

Constellations of the zodiac

Constellations are groups of stars that form a pattern in the sky. The zodiac is a belt of constellations along the ecliptic. Astronomers use these constellations to track the movement of the Sun, Moon and planets.

If you have heard of horoscopes, you might know the names of twelve of these constellations: Aries, Taurus, Gemini, Cancer, Leo, Virgo, Libra, Scorpius, Sagittarius, Capricornus, Aquarius and Pisces. But did you know that astronomers really mark thirteen constellations along the ecliptic? Tucked between Scorpius and Sagittarius is Ophiuchus.

Summer Solstice

Autumnal Equinox

CELESTIAL EQUATOR

ECLIPTIC

Vernal Equinox

CELESTIAL EQUATOR

Autumnal Equinox

ECLIPTIC

Winter Solstice

November

October

September

August

July

June

LIBRA

VIRGO

LEO

CANCER

GEMINI

Earth

The Sun

December

January

February

March

April

May

SAGITTARIUS

CAPRICORNUS

AQUARIUS

PISCES

ARIES

TAURUS

THE SHAPE OF TIME

If you were asked, "What's an example of 'time'?", what would you say? You could say that time is a period, such as the Bronze Age or the Middle Ages. Time can be a millennium, a century, a decade or a year. We can divide this even further: months, weeks, days, even hours, minutes and seconds. But *how* did we come to divide time in this way?

Time looks like . . .
For some people time is linear, like an arrow, stretching from the past and pointing to the future.

For others it is circular, meaning that all things will eventually repeat themselves. Many ancient civilisations saw time as a repeating cycle, as they observed the patterns around us:

. . . the seasons always circling . . .

Day turning into night . . .

The annual flooding of the Nile river was so important to the ancient Egyptians that they based their calendar on it.

The end is the beginning

Observing these repeating patterns of nature, some cultures concluded that the Universe itself would repeat in cycles. The cycles were made up of three phases: creation, use and destruction. After each cycle, creation would begin afresh. The Nahuas, a group of indigenous peoples from what is now Mexico and parts of Central America, believed that in the fourteenth century this had already happened four times.

Nanahuatzin is the humble Nahua god serving as our Sun today.

A beginning ... and an end!

The linear perception of time comes from the traditions of religions such as Islam, Judaism and Christianity. In these traditions, time began when a single God created the world, and one day God will end it.

This is where the tradition of using BCE (Before Common Era) and CE (Common Era) comes from, as it was originally based around the birth of the Christian figure Jesus Christ on this forward timeline. His birth started the Common Era and anything before his birth used to be called BC (Before Christ).

This is also the reason many places refer to centuries in the way that they do, for example the twentieth century referring to the 1900s. This is because the 'first' century CE was year 0 through year 99.

... annual weather patterns, such as droughts ...

... or monsoons.

Which version of time sounds most interesting to you: looping and connected cycles or an arrow pointing ever-forwards?

DIVIDING THE YEAR

The rhythms of the Sun and Moon play an important role in human calendars. But neither lunar nor solar time are as simple or precise as we might think! Let's look at bit closer at these two views of time.

Lunar calendars

Lunar calendars are the oldest in the world. Most start with a new moon or crescent moon, though lunar calendars from ancient India and Tibet started with a full moon. The ancient Greeks, Egyptians and Chinese all used lunar calendars. The Islamic (Hijri) calendar is an important lunar calendar used around the world today.

Solar calendars

Solar calendars developed over centuries based on the needs of farming societies, such as the Maya and ancient Egyptians, who used the seasons to plan their cycles of planting and harvesting.

Many cultures organised their societies using the Sun, but they all experienced problems because a solar year is 365.2425 days. 'Calendar drift' will happen if that .2425 is not adjusted for. Calendar drift is when dates start to move across the seasons bit by bit – a common problem in earlier times.

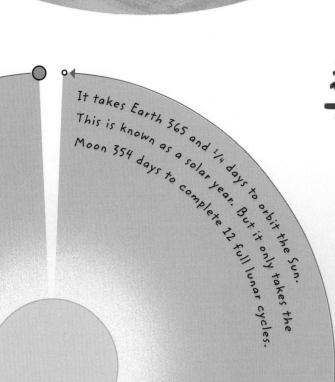

It takes Earth 365 and 1/4 days to orbit the Sun. This is known as a solar year. But it only takes the Moon 354 days to complete 12 full lunar cycles.

Leap to the Rescue

Today, the Gregorian Calendar is used by many different cultures around the world. To get around the problem of the extra ¼ day of a solar year, this calendar has a leap year added once every four years to synchronise it with the astronomical cycles. This adds an extra day, 29 February, known as a leap day. It's certainly an interesting day to be born, as it only occurs once every four years!

Many, many calendars

The Gregorian calendar might be widely used today, but not every country uses it to organise the year. Ethiopia and Nepal use their own unique calendar. Iran and Afghanistan use the solar Hijri calendar. Saudi Arabia uses the lunar Hijri calendar alongside the Gregorian calendar. Many countries adopt two or more calendars, one for civic life and another for religious practice or traditional events. This happens, for example, in Bangladesh, Egypt, India, Iraq, Israel, Libya, Myanmar, Pakistan, Somalia, United Arab Emirates and Yemen.

The Muslim festival of Ramadan is a good way to understand the difference between the solar and the lunar calendar. A year of 12 lunar months has 354.36707 days, whilst a solar year has 365.2425 days. As a result, Ramadan happens about 11 days earlier each year according to the Gregorian calendar.

Best of both calendars

Lunisolar calendars bridge the difference between the solar year and the lunar year. They use both the Moon and the Sun to calculate the date. The Jewish people were the first to successfully use a lunisolar calendar based on these calculations. Hebrew, Buddhist and Hindu calendars are all lunisolar.

BUILDING BLOCKS OF TIME

Have you ever stopped to consider why we have seven days in a week and 24 hours in a day?

Unequal hours of day and night

A day is based on one full rotation of Earth on its axis. The Babylonians, who lived more than 4,000 years ago near the equator, in modern-day Iraq and Syria, divided the day into 12 hours of lightness and 12 hours of darkness based on their experience.

But further north or south, the amount of daylight varies throughout the year. There are more daylight hours in the summer, and fewer in the winter. To deal with this, ancient Greeks and Romans used temporal hours, or unequal hours. This means that daylight hours in summer are longer than the daylight hours in winter.

This is what a modern watch face with summertime temporal hours could look like:

Night hours

Sunset

Sunrise

Day hours

Summer in the north

Near the equator, daytime is always about 12 hours long

Summer in the south

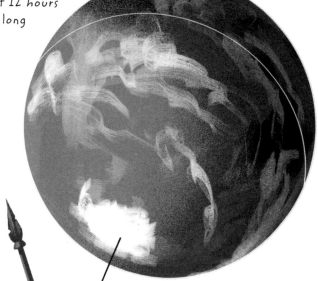

Long days in the north and short days in the south

Short days in the north and long days in the south

Seven days and seven nights

A week is a funny thing. It is the only time measurement not based on astronomical cycles. But it has been used by people around the world for thousands of years.

The ancient Babylonians worshipped the number seven. In Judaism and Christianity, God made the world in seven days. The Romans, following ancient Babylonian tradition, named the days of the week after the celestial orbs they saw in the sky:

Sun = Sunday
Moon = Monday
Mars = Tuesday
Mercury = Wednesday
Jupiter = Thursday
Venus = Friday
Saturn = Saturday

You might wonder where the planets Uranus and Neptune are. These planets are not visible to the naked eye, so when the days of the week were named, nobody knew they existed!

Mars

Venus

BODY CLOCKS

Life on Earth is influenced by celestial patterns in other ways, too. The light and energy of the Sun is crucial to all life on Earth. It plays a big role in many small ways throughout a day.

Natural rhythms

If you wake up early and are full of beans first thing in the morning, then you are likely to be an 'early bird'. If you prefer to wake up late and are a ball of energy in the evening, then we'd say that you are a 'night owl'. Whichever you are, this is called your chronotype.

These patterns are formed by your circadian rhythm – your natural or biological clock. Circadian rhythms affect your body's hormones, temperature and eating habits. They determine when you feel alert and when you feel sleepy. Your circadian rhythm will change as you grow.

Animal behaviour

Animals have circadian rhythms, too – that's where the phrases 'night owl' and 'early bird' come from!

Many animals, such as butterflies and songbirds, have diurnal internal clocks, like us. This means that they are active during the day.

Other animals are nocturnal and like to come out at night. Foxes and owls are good examples.

If you have a pet rabbit or hamster, you might have noticed that they are more active during the twilight hours. These animals are known as crepuscular animals – they prefer dusk and dawn to any other part of the day. Small prey animals are crepuscular to avoid predators. Other crepuscular creatures might use these hours to avoid hot, daytime temperatures, as in desert regions.

Starling murmuration

Moving with time

Starlings and other birds use the position of the Sun to navigate and time their annual migration. Like other animals, they can sense changes in the length of the day throughout the year. These instincts tell them when to migrate or hibernate.

Screen confusion

Many believe that screen time can interfere with your biological clock. The light from a screen sends signals to your brain telling you it's daytime, even late at night, when you should start feeling tired. This is why it is better to avoid screens and bright lights a few hours before bedtime.

EARLY TIMEKEEPING

The human body is an amazing machine capable of performing thousands of tasks all at once, but it is not so great at accurately measuring time. Instead, we have made all kinds of instruments to measure time for us. The first were made by our ancestors thousands of years ago.

Shadows and stars

Sundials are timekeepers. They rely on the Sun to cast a shadow on a surface marked with times of the day (so sundials do not work at night).

The oldest-known sundial was discovered by archaeologists in the Valley of the Kings, Egypt, in 2013. It is more than 3,500 years old.

The largest sundial in the world is in Jaipur, in India. It is 27 metres high and about 300 years old.

Ancient Chinese sundial

Nocturnal

Nocturnals, in contrast, can tell time at night. They were invented in the Middle Ages and showed the time based on the positions of the stars in the sky.

To use a nocturnal correctly, you had to set it to the correct date, find the Pole Star through the middle hole, and align a pointer to one of the stars in the constellation of Ursa Major.

Water, fire and sand

Some of the oldest-known devices for measuring time are **water clocks**. A bowl with a small hole in it slowly releases a stream of water into a container below. We can tell how much time has passed by checking the level of the water as it moves from one bowl to the next. (There was the problem of evaporation from heat or freezing from cold, however!)

Ismail Al-Jazari, a brilliant Muslim polymath, illustrated the most incredible and complicated water clocks in CE 1206. This elephant clock is just one elaborate example.

Al-Jazari's design for an elephant-shaped water clock

Incense clocks originated in India, but became very popular in China in the first century CE. Rolled incense sticks were carved with notches, then lit. As the notches burnt away, you could measure the passing of minutes, hours or days. Some also burnt through strings, dropping balls to make a noisy signal.

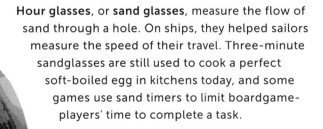

Hour glasses, or **sand glasses**, measure the flow of sand through a hole. On ships, they helped sailors measure the speed of their travel. Three-minute sandglasses are still used to cook a perfect soft-boiled egg in kitchens today, and some games use sand timers to limit boardgame-players' time to complete a task.

MECHANICAL TIME

The first **mechanical clocks** were invented in the thirteenth century, towards the end of the Middle Ages (CE 500 to CE 1500), but they were inaccurate timekeepers. They had only an hour hand and might run more than fifteen minutes fast or slow each day. Clockmakers, astronomers and mathematicians worked hard to improve their timekeeping.

Public clocks

In the early days of mechanical timekeeping, most people didn't have a clock to tell the time at home, so a central clock tower was a key part of a community. In towns and villages, ringing bells from a clock tower would indicate the start or end of gatherings and markets.

Cogs and gears

Early mechanical clocks had three parts. A driving force, such as a weight or spring, would keep the clock going. The cogs or gears would transfer the force to turn the hands. Finally, a special part called the escapement would keep the wheels turning at a regular pace.

In most clocks, something called a foliot was used to regulate the hands. This was a rod with little weights at the end that swung back and forth. But this was not very accurate, as their uneven swing made the clocks run too fast or too slow.

Foliot

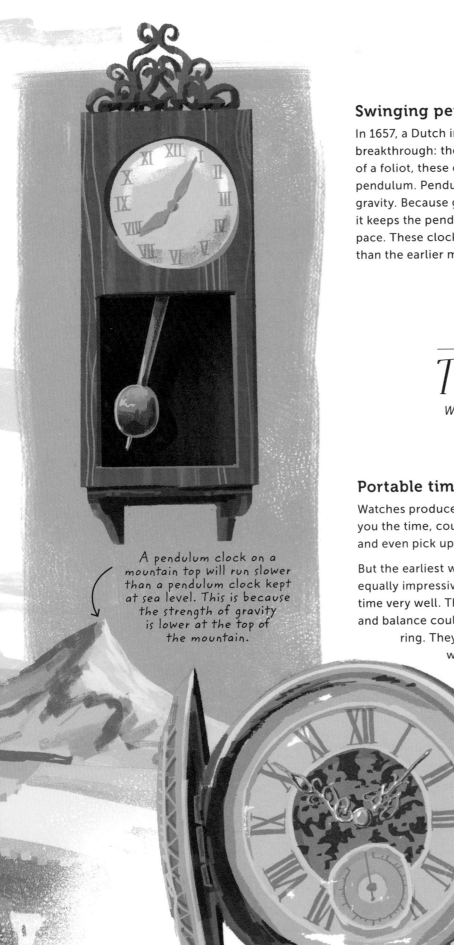

Swinging pendulums

In 1657, a Dutch inventor came up with a huge breakthrough: the pendulum clock. Instead of a foliot, these clocks were regulated by a pendulum. Pendulum clocks are controlled by gravity. Because gravity is a constant force, it keeps the pendulum swinging at a regular pace. These clocks were far more accurate than the earlier mechanical clocks.

The word clock comes from the Latin term clogga, *which originally meant 'bell'.*

A pendulum clock on a mountain top will run slower than a pendulum clock kept at sea level. This is because the strength of gravity is lower at the top of the mountain.

Portable time

Watches produced today are incredible. They can tell you the time, count your steps, measure your heartbeat and even pick up your phone call!

But the earliest watches of the sixteenth century are equally impressive, even though they did not tell the time very well. The whole mechanism of spring, cogs and balance could even be made to fit within a tiny ring. They could be beautifully decorated, with engravings, rubies, diamonds and intricate enamel details.

DIVIDING THE DAY

What time do you usually wake up for the day? You might start your morning at 7.30 a.m., or would you say half past seven, or even half to eight? What are the rules for talking about the time of day, and are they the same everywhere?

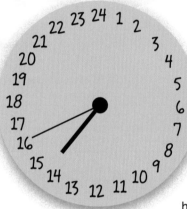

24-hour clocks and 12-hour clocks

A 24-hour dial displays the time from 1 to 24. The hour hand goes around the dial once in a day.

A 12-hour dial only has the hours 1 to 12. This means that on a 12-hour clock, the hour hand goes around twice in a day.

How we say the time is based on these dials. We speak of a whole hour when the minute hand points to the top and the hour hand to a number.

When the hour hand is not 'on the hour', we look to the minute hand to tell the time. The minute hand tells us how many minutes have passed.

Most dials have 60 small marks for each minute in the hour. At each number, 5 minutes have passed. That's why when the minute hand points to the 3 it means 15 minutes have passed since the whole hour. At 5, 25 minutes have passed, and at 10, 50 minutes have passed.

On this dial, the hour hand has passed the 3 and the minute hand is pointing to the 2. This means that 10 minutes have passed since it was 3 o'clock. But was it 3 in the morning or 3 in the afternoon?

a.m. vs p.m.

In some English-speaking countries, people refer to the morning as 'a.m.', and the afternoon as 'p.m.'. Both a.m. and p.m. refer to where the Sun is. The abbreviation 'a.m.' stands for *ante meridiem*, which is Latin for 'before midday'. The abbreviation 'p.m.' stands for *post meridiem*, which is Latin for 'after midday'.

But what about noon and midnight? Is noon a.m. or p.m.? If you write 12 p.m. for noon, someone might confuse that with midnight. But if you write 12 a.m. for midnight, someone else might think you mean noon! Many people advise to write 12:00 for noon and 24:00 for midnight to be extra clear. Or just say 'midday' or 'midnight'!

Midday/Noon

Afternoon

Morning

12:00

3 p.m.

9 a.m.

DAY

6 p.m.

Sunrise

Sunset

6 a.m.

NIGHT

3 a.m.

9 p.m.

Morning

24:00

Evening

Midnight

Half past or half to? Some languages, such as German, Dutch and Norwegian, prefer to use 'half to' the hour. It can become confusing if you drop the 'to' and speak of 'half seven' or 'half three'. If you are used to that meaning half past the hour you might find yourself an hour late!

TIME REDEFINED

For 250 years, pendulum clocks were the most accurate timekeepers the world had ever seen. But new developments in the twentieth century have changed our relationship with time for good. Time is no longer defined by the Universe around us, but by tiny atoms found on Earth.

Timing vibrations

The first quartz clock was a groundbreaking invention in 1927. But how does it work?

A quartz crystal vibrates when struck, just like a church bell or tuning fork, but much more steadily. Because this vibration is so stable, a quartz clock can measure time even better than a swinging pendulum.

Quartz timekeepers were also great news for sports. The Japanese company Seiko developed the world's first portable quartz clock, which was used to help keep time for long events, such as the marathon, at the 1964 Olympic Games in Tokyo.

Quartz crystal

Ethiopian marathon runner Abebe Bikila winning the gold medal in Tokyo, 1964.

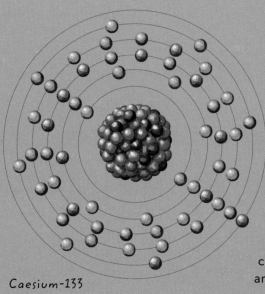

Caesium-133

Mind-blowing precision

The most accurate timekeepers in the world today measure time using atoms. Atomic clocks measure the vibrations of tiny atoms. Officially, a second is now measured as 9,192,631,770 cycles of radiation of the caesium-133 atom! Don't worry if you don't understand this, not many people do. But these devices really make us think about what time is and how we explain it.

Atomic clocks are very common now, even in space! For example, the United States alone has more than 30 satellites orbiting the Earth and each satellite carries more than one atomic clock. These clocks send signals to Earth that enable us to tell time and navigate.

All smartphones and smartwatches rely on atomic timekeeping or quartz technology. But atomic clocks are too big to fit on our wrists, so smartwatches today still use quartz crystals. The watches receive signals from the atomic clocks on satellites. These signals make sure that they show the correct time. Our watches and smartphones constantly communicate with their counterparts in space!

Some atomic clocks are so precise that they can measure time with an error of only 1 second per 300 million years.

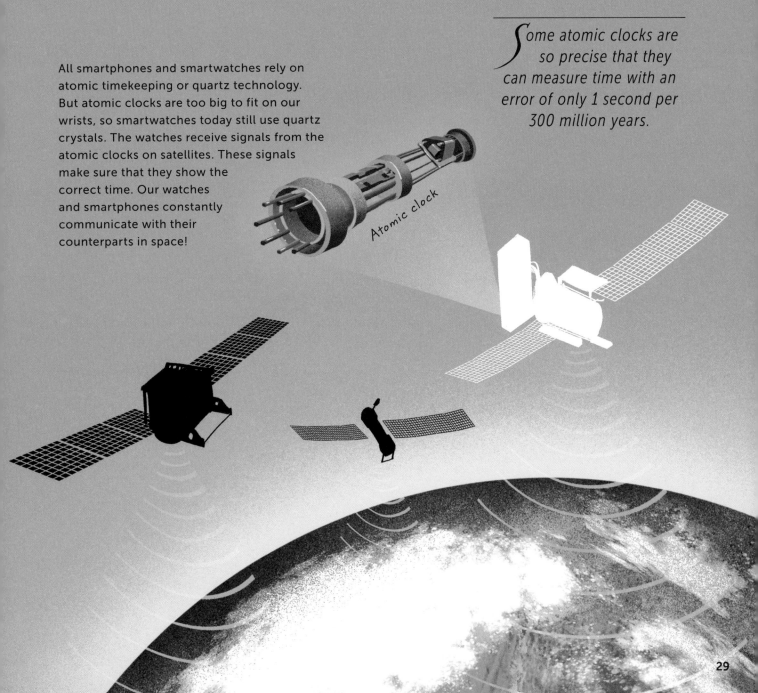

Atomic clock

WHAT'S THE TIME?

W e've talked about how water, fire, pendulums, quartz crystals and atoms are all ways with which we can measure time. But what they don't do is tell us how we know (or if we know) the time they're showing is 'right'.

When is noon?

You may be surprised to know that for most of human history, time varied between cities right next to one another. This is because our timekeeping was based on the movement of the Sun.

The middle of the day, or noon, is when the Sun reaches its highest point in the sky.

In the nineteenth century, towns and cities used the noon Sun to set their clocks to show 12 o'clock. This is called local time. This means that a clock set at noon in Tehran, in Iran, would not show the same time as a clock set at noon in Mashhad, even though both cities lie in the same country. This is because Tehran lies further to the west – noon occurs later for the people there.

Whose time do you choose?

A difference in time between east and west can cause problems. Let's say that a man from the eastern edge of Nigeria suggests meeting his aunt from the western edge of Nigeria in the capital, Abuja. If they met according to clocks set to their local Sun, the man would arrive 40 minutes earlier than his aunt, but both could claim they had the right time when they set out.

For centuries, humans did not worry too much about this and managed to get by using different local times. People did not travel as much as we do today, and travel, by horse or boat, was slow. When people travelled slowly over longer distances, they could gradually adjust to the local time of the places they were visiting.

A SPEEDY WORLD

It's only relatively recently that we've been concerned with clocks being in sync with one another. Before the 1850s, when travel and communication were slow, it did not matter that a clock in Chicago was set 55 minutes behind a clock in New York City. So, how and why did things change?

Speeding up

In 1800, a journey between New York City and Chicago took about six weeks. By 1830 the journey took roughly three weeks. Then, the construction of railways really sped up travel times and in 1857, the journey took just two days!

In the nineteenth century the pace of life soared in so many ways:

- Telegraph wires and electricity helped people send messages fast, over long distances.

- Railways connected towns and cities across countries and continents.

- Steamships and clippers moved goods and people around the world more quickly than ever before.

- Submarine cables laid on the seabed meant that messages could be sent instantly to another continent.

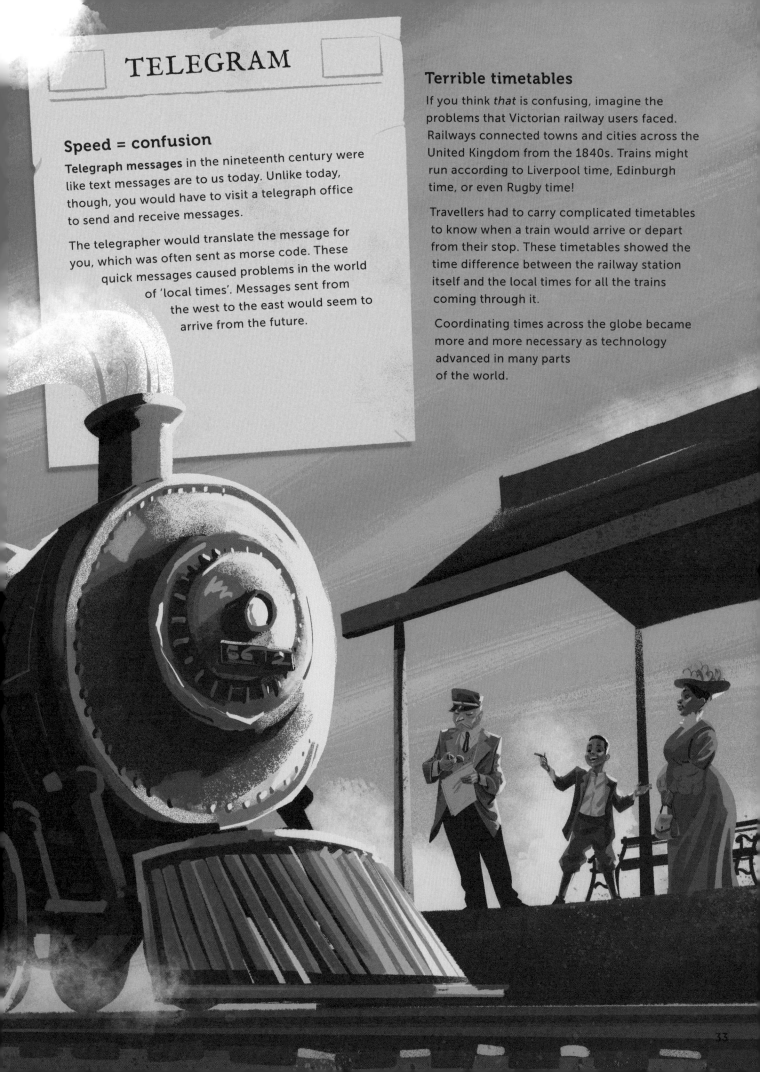

TELEGRAM

Speed = confusion

Telegraph messages in the nineteenth century were like text messages are to us today. Unlike today, though, you would have to visit a telegraph office to send and receive messages.

The telegrapher would translate the message for you, which was often sent as morse code. These quick messages caused problems in the world of 'local times'. Messages sent from the west to the east would seem to arrive from the future.

Terrible timetables

If you think *that* is confusing, imagine the problems that Victorian railway users faced. Railways connected towns and cities across the United Kingdom from the 1840s. Trains might run according to Liverpool time, Edinburgh time, or even Rugby time!

Travellers had to carry complicated timetables to know when a train would arrive or depart from their stop. These timetables showed the time difference between the railway station itself and the local times for all the trains coming through it.

Coordinating times across the globe became more and more necessary as technology advanced in many parts of the world.

33

Agreeing time

To make life easier in our connected and speedy lives, we now have time standards. This means that everybody agrees to use the same time within a region or a country.

Standardised time

Legal time is the time (or times) a region adopts as its standard. Any legal documents, such as birth certificates and marriage licenses, must use the region's legal time.

Greenwich Mean Time, or GMT, was the time measured by astronomers at the Royal Observatory in Greenwich, London. They used the stars and the Sun to determine the time, and a special clock to show this time. In 1880, by an

Act of Parliament, GMT became the legal time standard across all of Great Britain. By the early twentieth century, many countries based their own legal time on GMT.

Universal Coordinated Time, or UTC, replaced GMT as the world's time standard in 1972. It is determined by 400 atomic clocks that are held in over 70 national timing institutes around the world.

The Royal Observatory in London

Tweaking the system

Some countires agreed to do a synchronised clock change in certain seasons, to allow for more daylight at key moments of the day.

In 1810, the Cortes of Cádiz, (the Spanish parliament at the time) added regulations so that parliament sessions would start at 10 in the morning between October and April, and at 9 in the morning between May and September. They didn't change the clocks, but adjusted the time they started their day.

Daylight Saving Time (DST) is another example of shifting time to suit human life. In places that use this method, clocks are put one hour ahead in late spring and set back again in autumn for more evening light. This is why it is also known as 'Summer Time'. Summer Time can make people feel a little bit groggy at first, as it takes a while for our circadian rhythms to adjust.

The Cortes of Cádiz

Not every country keeps Summer Time. It only makes sense for countries further north or south of the equator, where the seasons and daylight hours vary most widely throughout the year. And not everyone who uses it likes it! Some people even protest about it as an outdated idea that is unnecessarily complicated for modern life.

TIME ZONES

It's easy now to find out the time anywhere in the world: we all use time based on UTC, so we can just do the maths. But how does it work on such a huge, global scale?

Noon at midnight?!

It is quite easy to standardise time within small countries, such as Bahrain, Luxembourg or Singapore. It is much harder to standardise time throughout the whole world. Imagine if the whole world kept the exact same time. This means that noon might occur at 3 p.m., or 7 a.m., or even at midnight in some places! And who would get to have noon at noon?

Instead, we use time zones, where each zone keeps the same time. In theory, time zones could divide Earth into 24 equal segments, with each zone running from pole to pole, and representing a one-hour difference in time. In the real world, though, this can't work, as continents and countries don't fit into straight lines.

Which time zone?

Instead, time zones follow other boundaries, such as the borders of countries or coastlines.

Central European Time includes many European countries.

Some countries are so large, such as Russia and the United States, that they use multiple time zones within their country.

Time standards across the world can be shown as plus or minus UTC. Countries that fall in UTC 0 include Ghana, Iceland, Mali, Portugal, Senegal and the United Kingdom. Some of these also use Daylight Saving Time for part of the year.

You should always check the time difference before you make a phone call to someone in another country in case you accidentally wake them up!

-12

-8

+11

-11

-10

Greenland
-3

0

Chukotka, Russia
+12

Alaska, USA
-9

-4

-1

-7

Iceland
UTC 0

NORTH
AMERICA

+11

-12

-11

-5

-2

THE INTERNATIONAL DATE LINE

-9

USA
-10 to -4

+1

-10

Mali
0

-12

-11

Panama
-5

+13

Costa Rica
-6

-4

-8

OCEANIA

SOUTH
AMERICA

AFRICA

-1

+12

Argentina
-3

Jetlag is caused by a disturbance to your circadian rhythm (see pages 20–21). If you have ever been lucky enough to visit a faraway country involving a long flight, you will know what jetlag feels like. You've been awake all day and at home, it's bedtime, but when you arrive at your destination it's morning! It might take a few days for your circadian rhythm to adjust itself to the local time in a new place.

-4

-12

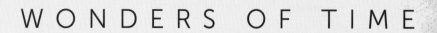

WONDERS OF TIME
LIFETIMES

So, humans can measure and standardise time, but what does it matter? How does this apply to our lives? How much time do we each 'have' in the grand scheme of the Universe?

The human world

The average lifespan of a human is 72 years. The oldest human being ever known to have lived was Jeanne Louise Calment, who was born in 1875. When she died in 1997, she was 122 years and 164 days old.

The wild world

Some species live even longer than we do.

Most of the longest-living animals can be found in the oceans.

Greenland sharks can live between 300 and 500 years; the childhood of a female shark lasts about 100 to 150 years.

Other impressive lifespans include that of the **red sea urchin** and the **bowhead whale**. Both can live to be more than 200 years old.

The oldest known **Galápagos giant tortoises** have lived well beyond 150 years.

But the most impressive must be *Turritopsis dohrnii*, the **immortal jellyfish**. As the name indicates, this type of jellyfish is potentially immortal. If injured, it can go back to a previous state of its life span and continue living. This does not mean all immortal jellyfish live forever. If they're not quick, they'll get eaten by something else!

Not all animals are this lucky. The poor little house mouse only lives for a year. The mayfly has even less luck — adult mayflies survive for only 24 hours.

3 million seconds of school

We all know how to use time to measure our ages. But how about other things? How much time do we spend doing things like eating, sleeping or going to school?

If you sleep for about 8 hours per night, about a third of each day, you will spend a third of your life sleeping. That's nearly 27 years if you live until you are 80!

Do you feel like you spend a lot of time in school? It's not really that long at all. The average time spent in primary school in a range of countries is about 779 hours per year. That's the same as 32 days. Or 46,740 minutes. Or nearly 3 million seconds!

You'll spend about 4.5 years of your life eating. You'll probably spend even more time watching television. TV time adds up to about 8.4 years for some people!

What's your favourite way to spend time?

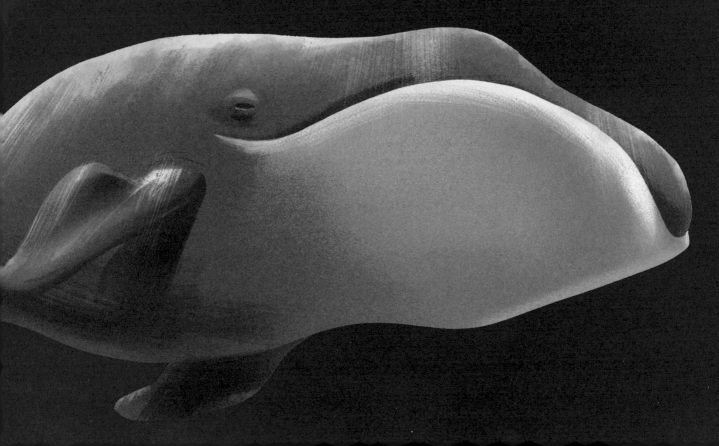

THE GOOD TIMES

Remembering all the great times we've spent in the past isn't always possible. Some people keep a diary to help them remember important events from their lives. But what about communicating with the future?

Messages from the past

Time capsules are a way to save and share moments in time. You can add anything you want.

Time capsules are often filled with newspaper articles and descriptions of important events, such as coronations or elections. But many people believe time capsules should be filled with details of everyday life and popular culture to fully represent the moment in time.

Humans have been making time capsules for hundreds of years. One was found in the buttocks of a statue of Jesus Christ, made in 1777 in Spain. Someone had put handwritten letters in the statue's hollow bottom. The letters described life in Spain, and they weren't discovered until 2017!

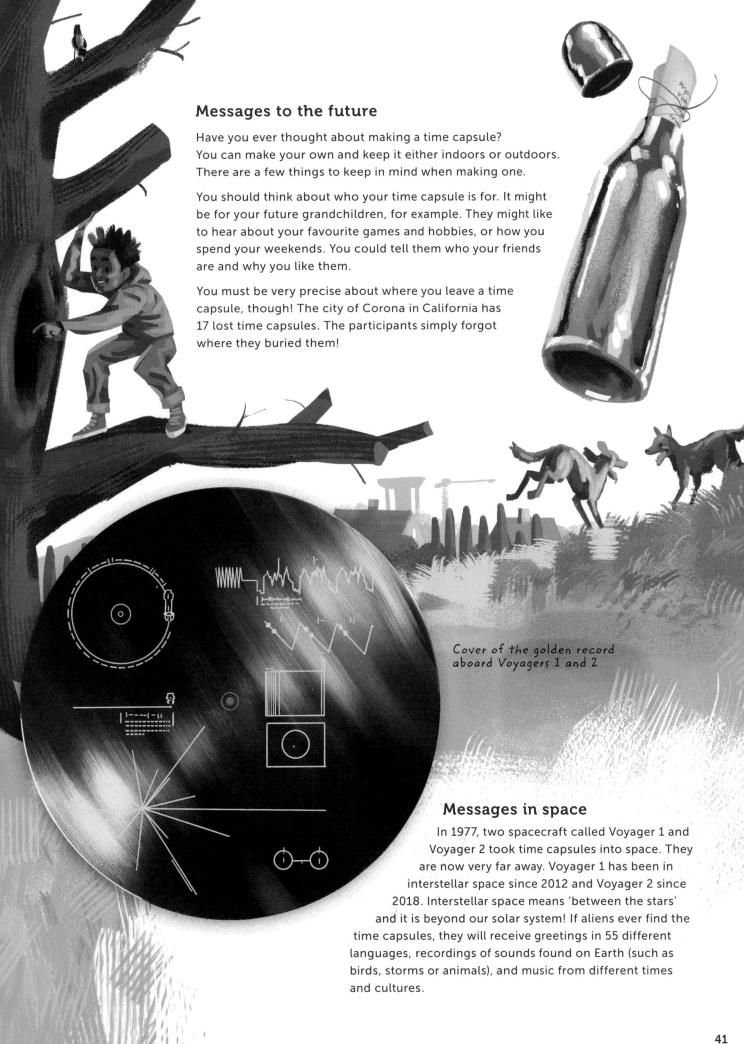

Messages to the future

Have you ever thought about making a time capsule?
You can make your own and keep it either indoors or outdoors.
There are a few things to keep in mind when making one.

You should think about who your time capsule is for. It might
be for your future grandchildren, for example. They might like
to hear about your favourite games and hobbies, or how you
spend your weekends. You could tell them who your friends
are and why you like them.

You must be very precise about where you leave a time
capsule, though! The city of Corona in California has
17 lost time capsules. The participants simply forgot
where they buried them!

*Cover of the golden record
aboard Voyagers 1 and 2*

Messages in space

In 1977, two spacecraft called Voyager 1 and
Voyager 2 took time capsules into space. They
are now very far away. Voyager 1 has been in
interstellar space since 2012 and Voyager 2 since
2018. Interstellar space means 'between the stars'
and it is beyond our solar system! If aliens ever find the
time capsules, they will receive greetings in 55 different
languages, recordings of sounds found on Earth (such as
birds, storms or animals), and music from different times
and cultures.

THE WONDERS OF TIME

Time is weird! We use it to organise our days and lives. The idea of time is embedded in our languages all over the world. We've created many sayings about time.

You can: 'have a whale of a time' or enjoy 'quality time'

'have time on your side' or find yourself 'racing against time'

be 'behind the times' or 'ahead of your time'

What do you think of the below sayings about time?

An inch of time cannot be bought with an inch of gold.

Time spent laughing is time spent with the gods.

Time builds castles, and time destroys them.

Man fears time, but time fears the pyramids.

Eat when the meal is ready, speak when the time is ripe.

Idle away, waste one's time.

What's your favourite saying about time? Mine is 'to lose track of time.' When that happens, it means I'm having fun!

While your experience of time will change from day to day and throughout your life, your clock or watch will continue to measure it at a constant rate. Or will it?

Travelling through time

Remember Einstein's theory of relativity? He said that time is relative.

Scientists tested Einstein's theory using atomic clocks and aircraft. They took four atomic clocks and put them each on a plane. The clocks had seats reserved for 'Mr Clock'. They flew around the world in different directions and landed back at the United States Naval Observatory.

The scientists then compared the flying clocks to the atomic clocks kept on the ground. The flying clocks recorded that less time had passed than the ones on the ground. This proved that Einstein was right, and that time goes slower the faster you travel.

What next?

So, what is the future of time? Nobody really knows. Some scientists are not even sure that time exists. Don't worry, though, they still believe our *experience* of time is real. This means that although we are unsure about how to define time in science and philosophy, we can still happily use it for our everyday lives.

We can't travel to the future or the past to find out, so all we can do is keep asking questions and learning.

Since the Big Bang, the Universe has been expanding. But will it continue expanding forever? And, if it doesn't, when will time end? Or will it all begin again?

AROUND THE WORLD IN
7 CLOCKS

A lthough most of us now have phones or watches, and no longer need to rely on public clocks to tell the time and organise our days, there are many clocks around the world that are worth a visit.

The Wishing Fish Clock in Cheltenham, UK, was designed in 1985 by Kit Williams, a children's author and illustrator. The clock tells a story. There is a goose that lays eggs, a fish that blows bubbles and a family of mice hiding from a snake! Its cast of characters includes Buttercup the Cow, Penelope the Pig and Purdy the Cat.

In Testour, Tunisia, you'll find the **Great Mosque of Testour**. Its minaret, a type of tower, is unique because it features a mechanical clock. Minarets, as clock towers once did, serve a religious function. From the top of the tower, the muezzin announces the time to pray. What makes the clock in Testour even stranger is that it runs backwards! And, stranger still, no one really knows why.

In a lovely house in the city of Blois in France there's a **mechanical dragon clock**. You won't find the time displayed on the front of it, but every half hour, dragons suddenly appear from the windows! The villa is a museum of magic founded in honour of the nineteenth-century illusionist and inventor, Jean-Eugène Robert-Houdin.

The Wishing Fish Clock

Great Mosque of Testour

Mechanical dragon clock

If you like puppets and storytelling, there is a great clock to go and see in Tbilisi, the capital of Georgia. The clock tower is next to the Rezo Gabriadze Theatre and some call it the **Leaning Tower of Tbilisi** because it looks as though it might fall over. Every hour, an angel emerges from the window of a balcony and rings a bell with a hammer. Below the angel, you'll see the 'circle of life' of a boy and girl.

If you are interested in the water clocks designed by Ismail Al-Jazari in CE 1206 (see page 23), then you can go and see a full-sized reproduction based on his drawings in a shopping centre in Dubai, United Arab Emirates. **The Elephant Water Clock** features a snake that dips forwards, a man who strikes a cymbal, and a bird on top that starts to chirp to mark the passage of 30 minutes or an hour.

The Leaning Tower of Tbilisi

The Elephant Water Clock

To see the largest mechanical clock in the world, you would have to visit Ganzhou in China, as that's where you'll find the **Harmony clock tower**. The clock faces are 13 metres in diameter and their minute hands are 7.8 metres long. That's about 5 times the average height of a 12-year-old.

The **Cosmo Clock 21** in Yokohama, Japan, is on one of the world's largest Ferris wheels. The wheel has a diameter of 100 metres. The time is displayed digitally at the centre of the wheel. This might be the only clock where people rotate around the dial like the hands on a traditional clock. Each rotation takes 15 minutes, so you would have to go around four times if you wanted to measure an hour!

Cosmo Clock 21

Harmony clock tower

GLOSSARY

atoms Atoms are the smallest building blocks of matter in the Universe. They are made up of tiny particles called neutrons, protons and electrons. Atoms form elements, such as hydrogen, helium and carbon. Together, atoms make up everything around us, from water and air to sand and rocks.

calendar drift This happens when a calendar does not keep time with the seasons. It was a problem with early solar calendars, such as the Julian calendar (used by the Romans), which was based on a 365.25-day year. This is slightly too long, and over a long period of time, the seasonal festivities would fall at the wrong time of year.

chronotype Your chronotype determines when you feel sleepy and when you feel alert. It might change throughout your life. Babies sleep a lot but often wake early. Teenagers often prefer to go to bed late and wake up late. But as people get older, they might start waking earlier again.

circadian rhythms These are natural patterns found in all kinds of living things. The 24-hour patterns are regulated by cycles of light and dark. These rhythms tell our bodies when to wake, eat and sleep.

crepuscular Describes animals that are active during the twilight hours. They prefer this to daytime or night-time. Some even come out later if there is enough moonlight.

Daylight Saving Time This is the custom – followed by many countries that lie north or south of the equator – of putting your clocks forward an hour for part of the year, to make better use of the sunlight in the summer evenings.

diurnal Describes animals that are active during the day. Most mammals and birds are diurnal, as are many flowers that open during the day. Humans are diurnal; we work and play during the day, and sleep at night.

ecliptic The ecliptic is the path the Sun appears to follow relative to the stars. The constellations of the zodiac can be found along the ecliptic.

escapement Together with the controller, the escapement forms a very important part of a mechanical clock and watch. Together they determine how fast or slow a clock is. They are still in use in mechanical clocks and watches today.

foliot A foliot is part of the escapement found in early mechanical clocks, used to regulate the hands.

Gregorian calendar The Gregorian calendar is used by many people around the world today. A standard year in the Gregorian calendar contains 365 days. Every four years, an extra day is added to create a leap year – an improvement on the earlier Julian calendar, to stop calendar drift.

interstellar space This is space between the stars. It starts where our solar system ends.

legal time, or standard time This is the time a country or region adopts as its official time. This means within a defined region, all clocks will show the same time.

local time This is the time determined by the Sun. It is noon when the Sun is at its highest point in the sky, but this varies depending on location. To avoid timing problems, we use standard time instead of local time.

nocturnal A nocturnal is an instrument that measures local time using the stars. Nocturnals were used from the Middle Ages until the eighteenth century by astronomers and sailors, to tell the time during the night.

orbit An orbit is the path that a planet follows around the Sun (or a moon around a planet).

polymath Someone who is good at many different things. They might be a whizz at languages and mathematics, play the trumpet and the harp, swim in the Olympics and lead the school sports team. Many prominent individuals in the past have been considered polymaths. This was often because they studied many subjects, rather than specialising in one, as we do now.

pendulums These are used in mechanical clocks as a controller. This helps them regulate the time that is shown on the dial. Because pendulums are regulated by the constant force of gravity, they are very good at keeping time.

speed of light The speed of light is an important measure in physics. It is the fastest speed at which anything can travel. The speed of light is a constant value, meaning it is always the same. It is exactly 299,792,458 metres per second. This is how fast light travels in a vacuum, or in space.

temporal (or unequal) hours These are hours that vary throughout the year depending on the season. They happen when a day is divided into 12 hours of darkness and 12 hours of daylight. Around the equator, the hours are roughly the same. But the further north or south you go, the more these hours vary during the year. During winter the day is divided into 12 shorter hours; in the summer, the day is divided into 12 longer hours.

FIND OUT MORE

BOOKS FOR TIME EXPLORERS

100% Get the Whole Picture: Space and Time
by **Paul Mason** (Wayland, 2020)

100% Get the Whole Picture looks at space and time through fun facts and stats, emphasising interesting percentages to put everything in perspective.

Astrophysics for Young People in a Hurry
by **Neil deGrasse Tyson** (W. W. Norton, 2019)

This book will tell you more about the science behind our Universe, from stars and supernovae to black holes and dark matter.

Comic Strip Science: Physics
by **Paul Mason** (Wayland, 2023)

Comic Strip Science: Physics makes learning about the science behind forces, energy and simple machines fun!

Everyday History: Telling the Time
by **Rupert Matthews** (Franklin Watts, 2000)

This book is great if you'd like to know more about the history of time and the instruments we use to tell it.

The Future of the Universe
by **Professor Raman Prinja** (Wayland, 2022)

The Future of the Universe starts the future clock NOW and rockets readers along a forward timeline that includes a shiny new ring on Mars, Earth's axis flip and a dramatic galaxy crash!

WEBSITES FOR TIME EXPLORERS

Space fun:
spaceplace.nasa.gov

If you want to learn more about the Universe, head over to NASA's spaceplace to learn all about space through online games and vidoes.

Science discovery:
www.natgeokids.com/uk/category/discover/science/

Here you can find all sorts of incredible facts about the way our world works – from the human body to outer space.

Hands-on science:
www.sciencekids.co.nz

This website has many resources to make science fun and engaging. Learn through games, quizzes, videos and experiments.

Taking astronomy further:
vimeo.com/royalobservatory/

The astronomers at the Royal Observatory have worked hard to teach you all about space. Learn all about 'Our Mighty Moon' or some 'Great Galaxies'.

Make a sundial:
www.starhop.com/blog/2020/4/16/at-home-stem-activities-make-a-simple-sundial-tk54y-khjr7

If you've always dreamed of making a sundial, here's how to do it!

INDEX